T0149364

ASCENSION

ASCENSION

A BOOK OF SONNETS

J A M E S   R .   D I X O N

Author of *Love, Attention* and *Affection*

ASCENSION
A BOOK OF SONNETS

iUniverse books may be ordered through booksellers or by contacting:

iUniverse
1663 Liberty Drive
Bloomington, IN 47403
www.iuniverse.com
1-800-Authors (1-800-288-4677)

Because of the dynamic nature of the Internet, any web addresses or links contained in this book may have changed since publication and may no longer be valid. The views expressed in this work are solely those of the author and do not necessarily reflect the views of the publisher, and the publisher hereby disclaims any responsibility for them.

Any people depicted in stock imagery provided by Thinkstock are models, and such images are being used for illustrative purposes only. Certain stock imagery © Thinkstock.

ISBN: 978-1-5320-1978-4 (sc)
ISBN: 978-1-5320-1979-1 (e)

Library of Congress Control Number: 2017905761

Print information available on the last page.

iUniverse rev. date: 04/18/2017

CHAPTER 1

Special

Because I'm a **MAN** I can't feel special
Where the hell are my flowers, my candy
My five star brunches, dinners with candles
My spontaneous gifts that are fancy

My pre-planned dates, trips, and activities
My random phone calls to say "I love you"
Why don't you ignite our intimacy
I pledged ninety-eight percent to your two

Maybe I should stop providing you with
Such immoderate standards of living
So I don't mistake your intentions with
Gold-digging tactics and false beginnings

How do I look at you as my equal
When your laziness shows we're unequal

Stars

When in love, I'd see stars in the day time
When connected, they spelled hers and my name
She'd say things; made my heart sing like wind chimes
I'd give it all to make her feel the same

I could see my whole future in her eyes
But she couldn't see her future in mine
She lacked attentiveness and compromise
She swindled me! She saw I had no spine

She took my dignity and self respect
Some would argue I handed them to her
My self-esteem I'll no longer neglect
I must love me first! Even she concurs

The stars that spelled our names were misleading
I won't be played or duped my next meeting

Senryu Intermission

Some women
love to say
"relationships are 50/50".
Really?!

Based on my personal experiences, women are selfish and codependent. However, I absolve them of half of the blame. The whole time they took advantage of me, I didn't do much to uphold my morality.

Love

He wants love! But what did she really want?
Love, companionship, friends with benefits
A piece of arm candy that she could flaunt
Her bad etiquette thwarts a genesis

Clearly he was a temporary fix
Flavor of the month; chewed up then spat out
Egg on his face bright like lemon cake mix
Dumped cold! The next day she took his friend out

Treacherous, devious, spiteful she was
Yet, he blamed himself for her transgressions
Through intimacy he thought he found love
The search should be deeper than affection

He wanted love! What did he get instead?
A debouched woman who left him for dead

Heartbreak

Moving on was hard. She was his first love
She was his first love and his first heartbreak
They shared ardent kisses and wistful hugs
Mourning the loss of her made his heart ache

For what it was worth, she offered friendship
Would that be enough? What if he wants more?
Still in love, he wanted companionship
But that's not available anymore

They just had to part ways for the better
To heal the wounds they've inflicted on us
Won't stay tied to his feelings like fetters
Then maybe they'll coexist and not fuss

Hopefully things will get better with time
As he digests her parting words "you're fine"!

Senryu Intermission

Friendship, companionship,
love, heartbreak, mourning.
Is this how love should be?

Failure in many forms makes me question the intentions of others. Failure to secure a long term relationship makes me question my intentions. Are relationships worth fighting for anymore?

Mirror

You'll need me before I **EVER** need you
Yeah right! That almost sounded convincing
That self fulfilling prophecy I use
To avoid dealing with my true feelings

I pressured you to be what I needed
Although you lacked substance, passion, and heart
My patience for you was unimpeded
I used you to fill a void in my heart

I fought fire with fire and still came up short
The answers to my problems start with me
I used you for emotional support
I deceived you and for that **I'm sorry**

Foggy, smoky, blurry; vision unclear
It's hard to look myself in the mirror

List

I'm discarded because I fail to meet
Each criteria of your ideal man
I'm not 6'5, or built like an athlete
I'm not a stud, or juicehead with a tan

I'm warm, fun, outgoing, and resourceful
I'm respectful, kind, loving, filled with bliss
I'll provide for you. I'm very thoughtful
But none of those qualities made your list

Superficially, I'm not meant for you
Surely you **need** me! Yet you deny me
Why? Do you feel like I'm too much for you?
Or maybe you're just not enough for me

I've settled for less than what I deserved
No longer will I continue to serve

Senryu Intermission

*Confusion, bewilderment,
disorientation* sums up
my thoughts

I was told I needed you! I was convinced life without you would be miserable! Every time I was presented with an out, I stayed. I stayed and sacrificed only to inherit misery.

Distance

Admiring your captivating beauty
You're physically close, yet mentally far
Women of your stature don't notice me
It hurts to mull reasons why we're apart

When we'd make eye contact my knees got weak
I'd dress good; spray extra cologne for help
I'm shy! I'd smile! Wouldn't attempt to speak
I'd do everything except be myself

Interacting with the opposite sex
Is frightening like a horror movie
Trembling and hunched as our paths intersect
My thoughts of approaching you are gloomy

Our kinship could be met with resistance
The safest move is to keep my distance

CHAPTER 2

Lioness

A strong lioness will protect her cub
Hold it tight so it won't feel neglected
Where was his lioness? Where was his love?
You **tormented** him; didn't regret it

A strong lioness will protect her cub
Aid them, guide them, be a symbol of strength
Where was his support? Where were all his hugs?
You pushed him away farther than arms length

He's unsure where they stand. Things need to change
They're like acquaintances. Things are discrete
Every day will be the same circle game
Just so you know, that's all it'll ever be

He tried to buy your love and affection
It was met with anger and retention

Stranger I

What are some things you enjoyed as a kid?
What outings did you plan on the weekends?
What's the name of the first guy you've dated?
Did you struggle in ways he did with friends?

More simple than that, where did you grow up?
What schools did you attend? Did you play sports?
What things motivated you to wake up?
You have malice towards him. What's the source?

He knows nothing more of you than your name
You might as well be a stranger to him
After over two decades, nothing's changed
Your absurd logic hurts you more than him

You're emotionally closed off; silent
A mystery! Just a **stranger** to him!

Senryu Intermission

I don't know you!
You don't know me!
At this point, does
it even matter?

When you'd extend your arms for a hug, I'd cringe out of
discomfort. You claimed I have a destructive attitude. I wonder
where I got it from. When confronted about our similarities,
you'd deny as if you're so much better than me.

Mannequin

Hard, 3-D, inhuman figure unmoved
Stiff body, absolutely no motion
Stillness in the eyes; cold, dark, and unbruised
Stoic look on its face; no emotion

I cried to you about my depression
But you don't extend your arms for a hug
I'm sad! You see my facial expressions
Still no emotion. You don't even shrug

My life is in a state of regression
Soulless at heart; I can't beg you to care
My pain, heart, life was in your possession
In return, I got an aloof, blank stare

Tense, graceless, 3-D statue like figure
Emotionless like a still shot picture

Control

You snap at him with ruthless aggression
About who he dates, befriends, how he eats
You try to control every decision
Dress code, career, how he spends his money

Listening to you made you feel proudest
You'd yell and fuss to mask your own issues
You're the Chihuahua that barks the loudest
With a bite soft like Cottonelle tissue

He's no codependent man. He's spent years
Cleaning the results of your bad advice
Cost him a lot of *blood*, *sweat*, *stress*, and *tears*
He paid that price. You can't control his life

You're **WEAK**! His success makes you **powerless**!
You've been stripped of all control. You're **jealous**!

Senryu Intermission

Needless to say,
he's developed a
tolerance to your
childish ways

The way you threw your weight around, you were a bully. You
tried so hard to rule with an iron fist with a hand full of nubs!

Stranger II

Who was your first crush? Who was your first love?
What's the nicest thing someone's done for you?
Who's the first guy you've ever kissed or hugged?
Tell me some funny stories about you

What were your career goals? Did you lose faith?
Who did you call on when life knocked you down?
You're crushed! What adversity did you face?
Where would you begin to turn things around?

Bottling up your childhood separates you
Your best teachings can be drawn from your past
Therapy could help if you'd share the truth
Your relationships could be better fast

Your lack of emotion hurts you and him
You're distant, vague! Still a **stranger** to him!

Never

You've never had a problem being **cruel**
Insulting him, calling him a loser
Placing bets that he would flunk out of school
Telling your friends "he's a bum, a failure"

You've never had a problem being **rude**
Mocking, harassing, chastising his friends
Acting like a self-righteous, stuck up prude
Saying he'll be strung out on drugs like them

How do you expect him to respect you?
Look up to you, follow your example
Every fiber of him **LOATHES**, **RESENTS** you
There's good in you somewhere. Give a sample

There are so many questions unanswered
Will things ever get better, unhampered?

Senryu Intermission

His heinous thoughts
suggested he wanted
to see you suffer
and grieve

Leave you fragmented, hurt, and isolated in your own misery.
Serve karma to you on a silver platter for everything you've done
to him. The logic behind the abuse and slandering is what he has
yet to discover. Because of that, till this day, their relationship
continues to suffer.

Narrative

You abused him **verbally**, **profanely**
Pissed on his dreams, shitted on his future
You then assaulted him inhumanely
You said "you're a disgrace and a loser"

"Your chances to gain success are finite"
"You **SUCK**! You're not the least bit athletic"
"You're **PATHETIC**! You won't amount to shit"
This was all love the way you foreseen it

Should he still fight to have you in his life?
The negatives outweigh the positives
Your tongue is sharper than a butter knife
Is it too late to change the narrative?

How much longer does he need to suffer?
When can their relationship be stronger?

CHAPTER 3

Skin

Scrapes, cuts, scars, bruises seemingly unreal
Hard to imagine he did this to you
Wounds bandages aren't strong enough to heal
You were the source of his anger issues

Slaps across your face. Punches to your arms
Kicks; late night phone calls for an ambulance
You meant fun, but he meant bodily harm
Playful banter soon led to violence

Rather than embrace the beauty within
You wear sweaters and scarves to hide your skin
Showing discomfort and embarrassment
Underneath your clothes lays beautiful skin

Break ups are hard! Moving on is harder!
You must forgive yourself to move farther

Senryu Intermission

Good, bad, or indifferent,
you never know
people's **TRUE**
intentions

When you invest an extensive amount of time, energy, and effort into trying to get close to someone, all you want in return is for it to be reciprocated. What you put into building a relationship isn't always what you get in return.

Stereotypes

Some unite over commonalities
Some lead whereas others follow. **I lead**!
Apparently I am the enemy
I'm verbally stoned to the point I bleed

Because I don't bar hop, club, smoke, or drink
I am the object of obscurity
Rather than judge, I embrace how you think
But your stereotypes disappoint me

Should I try again to be more like you?
Should I be content with being myself?
Should we meet in the middle? Start anew
Should we part ways? I'll look out for myself

I've tried your lifestyle; smoke, drink, clubs, parties
They've all had hazardous effects on me

Man

So I'm not good enough to raise your son
Hmm! But the man you replaced me with is
The man that you claimed loved you from day one
The man who cheats when you're five months pregnant

The man you'd call me to complain about
The man you bragged about to your mother
The man whom while you were pregnant ran out
The man you worshiped, praised like no other

The man your son now visits in prison
The man you placed on a high pedestal
He is **M-I-A** missing in action
While I'm still here, true and dependable

Your son could've had a real man to love
A man he could admire, respect, and trust

Senryu Intermission

You **PROMISED** me!
You promised things
will be different.
Again, **YOU LIED**!

Some decisions you make may benefit you in the short term.
Many of them have residual effects and have the tendency to
make your loved ones suffer.

Circus

Two kids, two different baby daddies
Both of which want nothing to do with you
One's on crack, the other ended badly
You led with sex! Two guys hit and left you

You came off fast, thirsty, and desperate
You have thrown yourself at me from day one
Because I rejected your advances
Now I'm public enemy number one

The life you've created makes me nervous
I can't date you based on that disclaimer
Sadly, your life is a three ring circus
You want me to be the lion tamer

I offered you friendship, support, and trust
Your motives and intentions were too much

Abnormalities

I'm *short*, *fat*, *non-athletic*, and I'm *weak*!
Now that we've exposed all my weaknesses
Let's talk about yours. You're **feeble**, you're **meek**
Insecure; you're mentally **dysfunctioned**

I declared you friend. You chose to be foe
With a muscular frame, you're so puny
Sinking into the abyss of your woe
At first you were winning. Now you're losing

Deep down it pains you to have to admit
You struggle to reach the bar that I've set
I wear pants while you wear skirts with a slit
You squat when you piss and I stand erect

You can't tear me down to build yourself up
NO! Simply put, you're just not strong enough

Senryu Intermission

You're your worst enemy!
It's **YOU**, not me.
I'm above you.
That **KILLS** you!

It took years, but I've finally figured it out. Does that make me more dangerous? Does your distain dislike for me intensify? You must really hate me now!

Fraud

You walk past me, ignore me in person
Yet later you request me on Facebook
Do I embarrass you? Are you burdened?
No smile, no greeting, not even a look

You like my posts; comment on my photos
Next day you act as if I don't exist
You send mixed signals. Are you friend or foe?
You're **shady**, **rude**! How could we coexist?

You claim you're my friend. Apparently not
Actions speak louder than words. Your actions
Says you're **FRAUD**! You're formulating a plot
I suggest that you write a retraction

I've seen twenty different sides of you
Which one is **real**? Which is **fake**? Who are **you**?

CHAPTER 4

Perfectionist

Mediocrity was just frowned upon
He'd vocalize all of his displeasures
ANGRILY like I was a dumb moron
He'd demand completion free of errors

His bone-chilling voice shook my foundation
Having me sit upright in a corner
Frightened! Knees tucked in fetal position
Awaiting his rude, scathingly torture

What if the shoe was on the other foot?
What if I **OBNOXIOUSLY scolded you**?
With your back pressed against the wall. Scared, shook!
Broadcasted your mistakes! Embarrassed you!

Why couldn't you just talk to me? Guide me
Have patience with me, teach me, inspire me

Scars

He was told he had more courage than brains
The cost of self expression was brutal
Belts across his backside piercing his veins
The abuse he suffered was still futile

His skin left a tapestry of bruises
To be viewed, displayed like a museum
A mere shell of himself. He felt useless
Bad, doleful; eyes welded up with rheum

Forced to grow up in abusive confines
He got the impression they hated him
Belts, straps, slaps, kicks. Those were just warning signs
He'd lay in his bed in pain with scarred limbs

Grown, but pre-developed with unhealed wounds
His day of reckoning has come too soon

Senryu Intermission

Every night he cried!
Headaches and nausea
resulted from dry eyes.

What was his motivation behind this? Could be years of pent up frustration that left scars on his heart tissue. Whatever the case, he has adopted those personality traits. Temperament, irritation, and frustration mixed in a bottle. With an M-80 fuse ready to flare at those who disrespect him.

Lost

Like most teenage boys, I was young, naïve
I tried to be like you. Tried to fit in
It appeared you had it all: *strength*, *reprieve*
Confidence, *guts*, *brawn*, *money*, and *women*

All things girls emphatically lust for
Those things ultimately made you suffer
I wanted everything you had and more
I lost the man I must rediscover

I did things astonishingly shocking
I disrespected girls, insulted kids
Thinking in the end you'd be proud of me
Now I have to live with those things I did

Like most teenage boys, I simply grew up
I'm done trying to fill your shoes. Grow up

Enemy

You taunt him, berate him, second guess him
Spewing nonsense when in your charged moments
You've made him your enemy once again
Don't underestimate your opponent

At age twelve, he wore earrings and loose clothes
According to you, that meant he was gay
If his growth didn't align with your goals
You'd threaten to disown him every day

All pride aside, he once idolized you
You verbally defecated on him
He defended your name! Others refused!
You paid him back by abandoning him

Biblically, he is to honor you
Although you've made it hard, he still loves you!

Senryu Intermission

You once told him
"we will go round
for round until one
of us gives up"!

You gambled your mortgage payments nearly rendering your
family homeless. You jeopardized people's safety with your bad
habits. **You're soulless**! You portrayed this image of provider.
You're bogus! You sold your friends out to indulge in your
cravings. **You're hopeless**!

Hoodwinked

You have harbored jealousy towards me
As my light shined, your light began to dim
You couldn't take it. Your peers praising me
Instantly, your legacy's forgotten

You're enthused with competing against me
But couldn't stand it when I'd beat your ass
All the mind games, bragging, chanting, taunting
Dissipated quickly! You have no class!

You thought you had the whole world by the balls
Thought you had us all bamboozled, hoodwinked
You're not fooling anyone. Not at all
You've caused more speculation than a shrink

I saw your true colors as a young teen
Others were too blind to see them. Not me!

CHAPTER 5

Dream

I dream so I don't see the disbelief
In everyone's eyes when they look at me
Owning my own business is a relief
Plus my high school and three college degrees

Yet I'm a general warehouse worker
Grad student and part time starving artist
Not much to show but scars from hard labor
Aged vehicle and one room apartment

Everyone has expectations for me
None greater than those I have for myself
The pressure, struggle, and stress, no one sees
No one understands! Just God and myself

It's hard to see what tomorrow will bring
Failure's good! Success hurts! That's why I dream!

Window

I'm looking out my apartment window
Windy, cloudy, foggy, rainy, stormy
Just watching mother nature crescendo
Hard to see anything. Even a dream

San Bernardino mountains filled with snow
Hills burned to ash from mysterious fires
Roads that lead to nowhere. Only God knows
Success is a tight rope; thin as a wire

The screen door view brings alluring nature
Plush green grass, pink roses, twenty foot trees
Views conducive to success, not failure
Through natural disasters lays my dreams

Behind the window is rain, lightening
Life beyond the window is enticing

Senryu Intermission

Those who aren't
secure with their
position try to stop
my growth, my shine

I'm completely aware of your body language. Reading my
resume makes your backside tighten up. Listening to me
verbalize my qualifications makes you squirm. Vocally, your
voice starts cracking. You begin to stutter as if you have a slight
case of amnesia.

Holidays

No greetings; everyone's an absentee
No text messages or phone calls from friends
Just me, a box of pizza, and ice cream
Alone in my dwelling till the day ends

No gift giving, or receiving. No cheers!
A lonesome soul forgotten, neglected
Spending the day off and on shedding tears
Just lying in bed binge watching Netflix

Maybe when I'm married and have children
I'll recreate Thanksgiving and Christmas
All I've lost and would love to have again
I'll regain tenfold every tradition

Holidays are miserable and sad
They all remind me of what I don't have

Birthdays

Everyone gathering to celebrate
With no essentials there's no point, no hope
No made invitations, cards, gifts, or cake
The guest list could fit on a post-it note

I out grew former, classmates, foes, and friends
Some are on drugs. Others are in prison
I have no children, wife, or a girlfriend
Birthdays aren't a cause for celebration

The posh red carpet gets rolled out for you
I question what am I celebrating?
Loneness, emptiness, depression, false truths
People partying while my heart's breaking

Birthdays and holidays I spend alone
With pizza and ice cream in my warm home

Senryu Intermission

Big family, lots of
friends, parties,
celebrations? But
at what cost?

I was lured into that trap once. Humiliation and embarrassment
awaited me at the front door. Is the lifestyle I dream about the
lifestyle I really want?

Pendulum

My heart's swinging back and forth; round and round
My mind says I don't want you in my life
My heart says I want you to stick around
But at what cost? How hefty is the price?

Thus far, all you've contributed was *stress*
Tension, hurt, pain, anguish, anxiety
Your spite caused my emotional distress
Your deviltry caused my PTSD

I forgive you, but I'll **NEVER** forget!
I love you! But I can't be around you
Only in small doses. That's all you get
Unless you finally tell me the truth

Back and forth, round and round, tick tock, it swings
Every second, minute, hour, day, it swings

Senryu Intermission

The deep end seems
shallow compared to
other waters that
I've swam in

Consistency is a personality trait damn near impossible to find
in someone. The aspersions people cast on a damaged soul can
be considered blasphemous.

Unravel

Relationships, friendships, flushed down the drain
I need you! Save me from my enemy
Deprivation, mutilation, scars, pain
Piercing my skin to see how deep I bleed

I went into a deep, dark hiatus
Shy man who views the world from his window
I felt like a plague, contaminated
While resting my head on a wet pillow

You've watched me unravel before your eyes
I need help beyond what you can give me
Some type of addiction to get me high
Maybe a prescription for therapy

Hurt and pain is not what you advertised
Peace, hope, and love is what you symbolize

CHAPTER 6

Ocean

There you are ninety yards from the crosswalk
Postcard like views: divine, peaceful, tranquil
From the roads, mountains, hills, pier, and boardwalk
You look beautiful from every angle

Cold waters, grazing warm liquid gold sands
Cool breeze slicing through heat to reduce sweat
I enjoy penetrating your wetlands
Relaxing with you! Watching the sun set!

I open up to you. Your voice soothes me
You're the antidote! Cure my depression
I'm confined, lost in your scenic beauty
You keep me calm; relieved from aggression

You're over thirty-six thousand feet deep
That's how much love I wish she had for me

Truth

"You're not six feet tall, strong, tanned with muscles!
You dress chic! You're too nice! You're a door mat!
You talk weird! Your stiff walk makes me chuckle!
You're chunky in the face; slight belly fat!

You have a job, a business, and degrees!
You elevate everything that you do!
You're supportive! You believe in my dreams!
You are NOT the man I'm accustomed to"!

At first glance, you've already tore me down
But you knew all this before you met me
But you still pursued me; jerked me around
Truth is, you're intimidated by me

Truth is, you don't feel you can contribute
Bring to the table the same things I do

Senryu Intermission

Rather than denigrate
or besmirch me, you
should elevate yourself

The victim routine is played out, outdated, and overrated.
Making excuses as to why you can't fulfill your relationship
obligations is more than pissing me off. I'm heavily
contemplating the significance of having you in my life.

Friends

My two former best friends were different
One's mother caused a divide between us
Made him compete with me in all we did
Drove him towards a life of crime and drugs

The other was self-indulged, entitled
He had it all: *money, gear, girls,* and *drive*
Comparable to a teenage idol
He could do no wrong; at least in his eyes

We were more than friends. We were like brothers
We knew all each other's likes and dislikes
Through good and bad times we backed each other
We bowled, traveled, pulled girls, had fights, lived life

I'd trade it all to relive the old days
Although I've had lots of success to date

Lighthouse

The abuse, the selfishness, spiteful acts
All of the embarrassment you've caused me
The yelling, fussing, violent attacks
The self-righteousness, power trips, and greed

All your failed attempts to get to know me
The incriminating, public shaming
Your failure to raise me responsibly
Your constant bitching, whining, complaining

I'm searching for peace and tranquility
I confide in you. I have no one else
No family, no friends. Just you and me
You're guidance will help me to love myself

I'm still questioning their significance
Am I fighting a battle I can't win

Senryu Intermission

You controlled me
like a puppet on
strings. You took
advantage of me

You hate the love, respect, and adulation I get. Now you're a
hypocrite. Now you're shining the pedestal you placed me on.
Bragging about my success from the choices you profusely
defecated on. Now you show me off like a monkey at a traveling
circus performing tricks and stunts to evoke your praise and
standing ovation.

Eulogy

We're gathered to lie to rest "**DEPRESSION**"
You left me scarred, bruised; laying in the wings
My mind, thoughts, soul was in your possession
You controlled me like a puppet on strings

You left me lying in my blood for years
Causing **misery**, **anxiety**, **fear**
Trepidation, **humiliation**, **tears**
Because of you, I questioned my place here

Before you rest in peace, I'll say thank you!
You left me a lifetime of memories
Yesterday, I stopped investing in you
Today, I started believing in me

You're **wrong**! I'm **right**! You can't **win**, I can't **lose**!
I'm not my worst enemy! Neither are you!

Senryu Intermission

Depression; my test.
There's only three
words that suit you best
"**Rest in Peace**"!

It took years, but I finally conquered you! I laid waste to the beast! Time to start anew!

New

New year, new me! New attitude! New dreams!
New motivation! New strength! New outlook!
New chance to wipe the slate clean! New beliefs!
New confidence! New therapeutic book!

Brand new look! New memories to create!
New friends! New morals! New values! New life!
New trials! New tribulations to face!
New relationship! Maybe a new wife!

New job! New career! New zeal! New lifestyle!
New car! New house with new white picket fence!
New family structure! New love! New smile!
New trips! New journeys to experience!

New year, new me! New mindset! New focus!
New approach to life! New heart that's open!

Previous Release

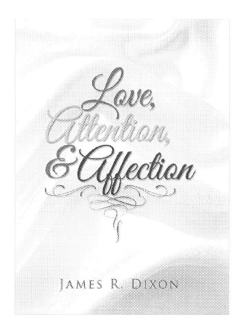

Love, Attention, and Affection is a three part story elaborating on my trials and tribulations in relationships. It is comprised of three individual stories. But, collectively the three stories combine to tell one ultimate story. Each individual story is represented by a particular color that generalizes the emotions and sentiments of the story. Love is represented by red. Attention correlates to yellow. Affection is strongly associated with purple. With this book I aspire to ignite healthy conversations with people as to what essential functions and components are necessary in order to obtain and maintain a successful relationship.

Previous Release

Broken Silence presents a collection of very personal poems that get to the heart of who author James R. Dixon is and what he has to say. He believes that sometimes the quiet ones have the most to say, but getting others to hear them can be a problem. Being different can mean that you may find yourself explaining your actions to others.

Broken Silence is also his breakthrough collection explaining his thoughts and feelings on relationships and other personal issues. These poems seek to offer hope and inspiration to others who are struggling to find themselves.

Previous Release

The Other Me presents a collection of very personal poems by author James R. Dixon. It is based on misconceptions placed on an individual's personality. He feels as though many people have been perceived a certain way by others and for the most part, those preconceived notions are wrong. With that said, that puts people in the position to have to defend themselves against those who misjudge them. "The Other Me" is his self-defense.

Printed in the United States
By Bookmasters